THE
Archive Photographs
SERIES

DAVENTRY

THE
Archive Photographs
SERIES

DAVENTRY

Compiled by
Barbara Hornby

CHALFORD

First published 1998
Copyright © Barbara Hornby, 1998

The Chalford Publishing Company
St Mary's Mill, Chalford,
Stroud, Gloucestershire, GL6 8NX

ISBN 0 7524 1069 5

Typesetting and origination by
The Chalford Publishing Company
Printed in Great Britain by
Bailey Print, Dursley, Gloucestershire

Contents

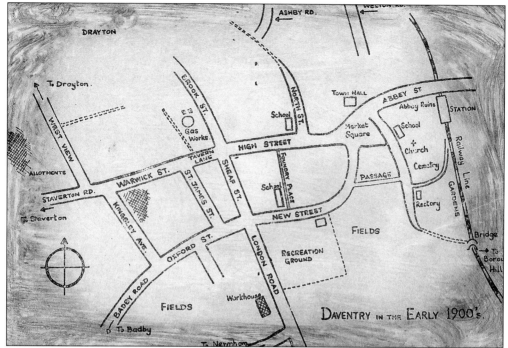

Map of Daventry in 1900

Introduction

Looking through a book of photographs is like watching a silent film. Because there is no sound, we have to look a little harder to work out what is going on and then we are transfixed by the details of what we see. These photographs of Daventry, carefully gathered by Barbara Hornby from a number of sources, are on the face of it typical survivals from an earlier age. But when we look more closely, we can see their distinctly Daventrian nature and the story of this ancient market town begins to emerge.

There have been regular markets in Daventry for probably more than 800 years. People from up to seven miles away would have travelled to the market to sell their own wares and buy what they could not produce themselves. There were livestock markets too and special fairs known as 'mops' where agricultural workers and domestic servants put themselves up for hire. The mops, being a natural break between one employment and another, were treated as a holiday with amusements and fairground rides. In this form they survived well into the twentieth century.

The last years of the nineteenth century and the first three decades of the twentieth can be seen as something of a watershed in Daventry's history. The stagecoaches which had brought so much business to the town were long gone, seen off by the railway. The London to Birmingham line opened in 1838, bypassing Daventry, and this new means of transport was so much quicker that travellers rushed to take advantage of it. Very soon, the only sign that Daventry had once been an important stopping off place for travellers was the number of coaching inns with their distinctive enclosed yards. Two of the largest of these inns have now found new roles, one as a building society and one as an old people's home, but the evidence is still there in the architecture. No traces now remain of the railway station, built when Daventry finally acquired a branch line in 1888. The last train left Daventry in 1958.

The whipmaking trade which was a local speciality had also gone by the turn of the century. Daventry now made boots and shoes, though never in such large quantities as other places in the county. However, Daventry was about to make its name in a completely different context. In 1925 the BBC began to erect a long wave transmitter station on the top of Borough Hill. For nearly seventy years, the Daventry skyline was dominated by a forest of masts and 'Daventry calling' carried the name of the town to thousands. In 1992 the transmitter station was closed and all but one mast taken down.

By this time, Daventry was several times larger than it had been a century earlier. It was now a modern town with industries, connected to the rest of the country by the nearby motorway network and to Europe via its international rail freight terminal. Designated an 'overspill' town for the people of Birmingham, the town underwent radical changes. But at the heart of the town there still lies a historic core - the church, market place, High Street and Sheaf Street are still laid out in a pattern established in medieval times, embellished with the architecture of later periods. It is to both the old Daventry and the changing Daventry which these photographs transport us.

Victoria Gabbitas
Curator
Daventry Museum

One
The Town

Houses in New Street (see p. 16). (see p. 16)

Aerial view of Daventry town centre taken in the 1950s. Note the railway station and goods yard at the top of the picture. Daventry was on a branch line of the LNWR from Weedon to Leamington. It is interesting to note how few people and cars there are on the streets, even at ten past two in the afternoon.

In Pigot's National Commercial Directory for 1830, Daventry was described as 'an ancient and respectable market town, borough and parish.... It was anciently spelled Daintree and is still provincially pronounced so'. The many fairs of Daventry were also listed, including one in early October 'for cattle of all sorts, and cheese and onions'. Also held in the Market Place were the 'mops' or hiring fairs. Considered a day off by the people looking for new positions, there was all the fun of the fair with roundabouts, swings and stalls. These traditions live on in the weekly markets still held today, although no longer in the Market Place.

Market Place and church, Daventry, *c.* 1900.

Market Place and Moot Hall, taken with the top view at the photographer's back, probably at about the same date. The Moot Hall, built in 1769, was originally a private house. It was bought by the borough when the first Moot Hall, which stood across the end of High Street and obstructed the entrance to the Market Square, was demolished in 1806.

The Moot Hall and part of The Plume of Feathers, early 1900s.

Across the street from the Moot Hall, early 1900s. Are the buildings being repaired or demolished?

Market Place and Moot Hall, now with the Burton Memorial which was erected in memory of Edmund Charles Burton (b. 1826), a very prominent figure in Daventry affairs, who died in 1907.

Another view of the Market Place showing the Peacock Hotel which used to stand on the corner of Cow Lane (now New Street) and the Market Place, 1932.

Overhead views, probably taken from the Church tower, of the backs of buildings along New Street, *c.* 1970.

New Street, looking toward the Moot Hall, 1960s.

New Street from the top of the police station, 1960s.

New Street, opposite the police station, 1960s. Note the Regal Cinema entrance in the second building from the right and the actual cinema hall behind the houses.

A closer view of the same, 1960s. The gentleman going into his house on the left is Mr Len Smith, returning home for lunch. Alfred Thornton, husband of Betty Thornton who lent these photos, was born in the house on the far right, next to the cinema entrance.

Park entrance on London Road. The date over the arch is 1910.

DVY .67F.   DENETRE HOSPITAL. DAVENTRY.

Danetre Hospital, London Road. Note the unusual spelling. This building was once Daventry workhouse.

London Road from the site of the present roundabout joining New Street, Sheaf Street, Oxford Street and London Road, in the early 1900s.

View of London Road from the same spot, *c.* 1909.

Traffic accident, at the same spot on London Road, in the early 1900s.

Turning 180 degrees, the view up Sheaf Street with the Wheatsheaf Hotel, early 1900s. Note the small size of the monkey puzzle tree which is now quite tall.

Sheaf Street, early 1900s.

Another view down Sheaf Street, mid-1900s.

Sheaf Street and the Marquis of Granby public house.

The corner of High Street, Sheaf Street and Brook Street in the early 1900s. William Hollis, hair dresser, is in the 1874 Kelly's Directory, but not in the one for 1903.

The same corner as in the upper picture, now showing the new or heavily renovated building on the corner of High Street and what was until recently the BBC Club on the left.

View down Tavern Lane at the junction with Sheaf Street, Brook Street and High Street, early 1900s. The BBC Club building is on the left and the bakery on the right. The bakery has now gone and the Saracen's Head is on the corner.

Brook Street, early 1900s.

High Street from the Sheaf Street end, early 1900s. W.B. Willoughby's grocery shop on the right was at 67 High Street. The message on the back of the postcard is from Mr Adams, printer of the postcard, whose shop was at 52 High Street, reminding Mr W.B. Willoughby who had been to Canada that he was to read a paper about his trip.

The Bear Hotel, High Street.

High Street, early 1900s.

High Street, looking down towards the BBC Club.

Allotments at the back of the Regal Cinema, between New Street and High Street, 1966.

Yard and air raid shelter behind No. 78 High Street and the Dun Cow pub on Brook Street, 1966.

Behind No. 29 High Street, once the Co-op, 1971.

Behind Nos 36, 38 and 40 High Street, 1966.

Norton Road, now Abbey Street, showing The Abbey Inn, the tall building on the left, in the 1960s.

The Abbey Inn, Abbey Street, 1920s.

Norton Road, now Abbey Street, 1967.

Another view of Norton Road in 1967.

North Street, showing the house now known as the Beehive.

Bishop Crewe's Hostel, North Street, 1915. This building, opposite the library, now contains offices. In his will of 1720, Lord Crewe of Steane, Bishop of Durham, left £6 a year for a charity school in Daventry.

Badby Road (note the misspelling), mid-1900s.

Badby Road (showing bypass), 1930s.

Waterloo from St James Street, early 1900s.

Waterloo, showing the gasometer.

Cottages in Waterloo opposite the Band Hall, 1960s. The man of the couple walking along the path is Mr Alfred Clare; judging by their clothes, they are on their way to a wedding.

Warwick Street.

Orchard Street, Drayton, early 1900s.

View of Daventry from Cherry Orchard, Drayton.

Two
Shops and Work

J.H. Ivens in his shop (see p. 36). (see p. 36)

Mr J.H. Ivens, wine, spirit and cigar merchant, and his horse sending Season's Greetings, 1910.

Mr Ivens in his shop on Warwick Street, *c.* 1910-16.

H.B. Kightley, baker and confectioner at 34 Sheaf Street, in 1900.

K. Marshall, baker, 2 London Road, in 1900.

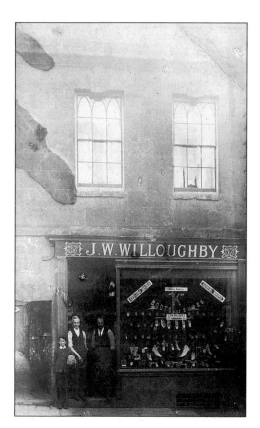

J.W. Willoughby's shoe shop, 57 High Street. Mr Willoughby is second from left. He was a well-known Methodist lay steward and father of R.J. and W.B. Willoughby. The shoe shop appears in both the 1874 and 1903 editions of Kelly's Directory.

'Gran' Eliza Harrisson (1844-1932) and her daughter, Emma (b. 1871), standing in the doorway of the shop in what is now 5-9 School Street, Drayton, c. 1905.

Gran Harrisson and her granddaughter, Toria Wood (b. 1911), standing in the shop doorway, c. 1927.

May Wood, Gran Harrisson's daughter, on the left, and her daughter, Toria Wood (later Willoughby), in front of the shop, c. 1930.

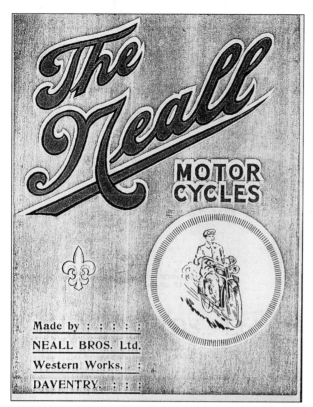

Brochure for Neall Bros Ltd, motorcycle manufacturers. The factory was in Foundry Place.

Cheshire and Berwick, motorcycle dealers, Sheaf Street. Mr Harold Berwick is the second from left (see p. 63).

Advertisement in the Daventry directory for The Golden Padlock, 1947. This building is now Lloyds Chemists.

J. P. OSBORN

PROPRIETOR L. B. BUTCHER

IRONMONGER : HARDWARE : TOOLS
PAINTS : HORTICULTURE SUNDRIES
ETC., ETC.

The Golden Padlock

27 HIGH STREET : DAVENTRY
Telephone No. 9

THE OLD MANOR HOUSE of Daventry, with its fine old Staircase, oak panelled Rooms and Tudor Fireplace can be shown to visitors on request.

Knife grinder in the alley near Stead & Simpson (now White's), 1960s.

Kath and Ernie Graham
in their sweet shop on
Brook Street. They were
much loved by the local
children.

Kath Graham blowing her horn in front of her shop on Brook Street, 1950s.

Jack Harding in front of his shop at 14 Sheaf Street, late 1950s.

Lasting and finishing room at Stead & Simpson's Daventry factory, 1920s.

Opening ceremony of the Daventry 5XX BBC station, 27 June 1925. The Postmaster General, Sir William Mitchell-Thomson, is in the centre holding his manuscript and the BBC's managing director, Mr (later Lord) J.W. Reith is standing behind him. The trolley-like device is the microphone.

An engineer adjusting an AT induction coil at Daventry 5XX, 1925.

Daventry 5XX wireless station, Borough Hill.

Empire wireless station, Borough Hill, 1948.

The canal near Daventry, early 1900s.

Daventry Special Constables, date unknown.

Three

Pubs and Inns

Garden of the Bear Hotel (see p. 55).

Yard at the rear of the Wheatsheaf Hotel, 1968.

In 1720, Daniel Defoe said '...then we came by Southam to Daventry, a considerable market town, but which subsists chiefly by the great concourse of travellers on the old Watling-street way....' Because of that 'great concourse' of up to eighty coaches a day, the inns of Daventry flourished and notices appeared regularly in the Northampton Mercury about the George, the Plume of Feathers, the Saracen's Head and the Peacock. The two greatest inns, the Wheatsheaf and the Saracen's Head, were more than just hotels. Their enormous stables housed the relays of horses needed for the post and stagecoaches. They offered a wide range of other services including banking, auctions and, at the Wheatsheaf, postal services. The Wheatsheaf, of course, is famed as having been the headquarters of Charles I before the battle of Naseby. At one time there were about thirty inns and pubs in the town but the arrival of the canal and then the railway brought about a change in Daventry's fortunes and those of her innkeepers.

Detail of stonework in the yard of
the Wheatsheaf, 1968.

Detail of stonework in the yard of
the Wheatsheaf, 1968.

The Plume of Feathers, Market Place.

Receipt from Phipps & Co. (Northampton and Towcester Breweries) Ltd, 8 High Street, Daventry (see p. 58).

The Peacock Hotel, on the corner of New Street and Market Place, early 1900s.

The Peacock Hotel in the 1930s.

The Plough and Bell, 48 New Street, early 1900s.

The Plough and Bell, somewhat later, now tidied up.

The Red Lion, Brook Street, 1924.

The Red Lion, 1932.

The Marquis of Granby, Sheaf Street.

The Second World War air raid shelter in Sheaf Street and cellars of the Marquis of Granby public house, which were unearthed during the construction of new shops off Sheaf Street near the post office.

Lion and Lamb Inn, High Street.

The garden of The Bear Hotel, High Street.

The Racehorse, Brook Street, 1940.

The George, St James Street.

Fox and Hounds, 23 London Road.

World's End, Sheaf Street, 1932.

The Royal Oak, Braunston Road.

Northampton Brewery Company
Stores, 8 High Street, which were
given up in 1925.

Four

Entertainment

Merry Comrades at the New Theatre (see p. 75).

Spectators awaiting the start of a race on Newnham Hill, 1906.

In the early days of the motor car and the motorcycle, Daventry became well known in motor racing circles mainly because Newnham Hill provided such an exciting venue. The Coventry Motor Club was the first to use Newnham Hill for hill climbing in 1905. In 1907, the Club paid to have the hill metalled to alleviate the dust problem. The hill was used until 1923 when the races moved from the road into the adjacent fields like the American hill climbs, thus introducing scrambles into the sporting agenda.

Weighing in at Daventry Railway Station for the Newnham Hill Climb, 1906.

Behind the starting line for the Newnham Hill Climb, 1906.

Mr A.E. Gould driving his 15 h.p. Humber in the hill climbing competitons at Newnham Hill, 1907.

The Coventry Motor Club motorcycle hill-climbing competition under way at Newnham Hill in 1908. According to the reporter, 'despite the large crowd... the events were run off without accident... Mr Phil Baker of Daventry finishing first in the class for single-cylinder motor cycles'.

Apprentices of the Rex Motor Manufacturing Company, Coventry, 1904. Harold Berwick is seated in the centre of the front row. Harold Berwick was born in Fenny Stratford and joined the Rex Motor Manufacturing Company in Coventry as an apprentice in 1904. As a qualified engineer, he started a bicycle and motorcycle shop in Daventry in 1919 and later built what became the Maple Leaf Garage. He obtained his licence to drive in 1907 and became a well-known racer and test driver for several motor manufacturers. He died in Daventry in 1957 aged 71.

Harold Berwick in 1906.

Harold Berwick in a 6 h.p. Rover, 1906.

64

Harold Berwick driving in the Isle of Man TT races, 1914.

Harold Berwick (in the right hand bed) in Nobles Hospital, Isle of Man, after an accident in the TT races in 1914.

Harold Bewick (second from right) and fellow riders from the Humber works team taking part in a trial on the Isle of Man.

Harold Berwick riding a Humber at the top of Shap Fell, 1912-13. He had been over Shap Fell before, having been the first rider to take a sidecar over.

Harold Berwick racing on Newnham Hill, 1912.

Miss Muriel Hind, later Mrs Lord, who rode Singer and Rex machines in competitions for many years. She is shown here with a 6 h.p. Rex in 1911.

Old Crocks and Scarlet Runners, 1897.

Daventry Early Closing Cricket Club, 1904 season. Back row, left to right: E. Cherry, S. Wiggins, S. Collett (Honorary Secretary), A. Sexton, W. Wareing, G.E. Bishop, E. Harris (Umpire). Middle row, left to right: Dr O'Rafferty (President), J. Wood (Vice-Captain), T. Dilks (Captain), W.H. James, T. Muddeman. Front row, left to right: H.D. Simpson, A. Gibbs, W. Collett (Scorer).

Members of the Daventry Road Club, *c.* 1932. Upper picture, left to right: Jack Truslove, Ivy Wright, Lewis Claydon, Edie Smart, Dick Ashwell and Dan Nightingale.
Bottom picture: third team prize winners, left to right: Dougherty, Nightingale, Truslove, Hulbert, Rigby and Ashwell.

Daventry Bowls Club, *c.* 1954 (below). On the back row at the extreme left is Bill Franklin, the fifth from the left is Harry Miller and the fifth from the right is Frank Tebbutt. On the middle row, the third from the left is R.J. Willoughby, the third from the right is A. Vogt and the second from the right is Bob Neal. On the front row, at the extreme left is Mr Neal (who owned a cake shop), the fourth from the left is Mr. Dodson (a headmaster) and the second from the right is Mr Moore (Town Clerk).

Daventry Butchers' Football Team, 1912-13. Back row, left to right: -?-, H. Emery, J. Smith, W. Smith, ? L. Linnell. Middle row, left to right: H. Weston, F. Stevenson, -?-, -?-, ? Elliott; Front row, left to right: -?-, ? Butlin, M. Andrews.

Crick Ladies' Cricket Team, 1969. Left to right: Mrs Smith, Rose Adnitt, Bertha Fox, Gwen Adnitt, Violet ?, Kit Herbert, Pam Cox, Marge Collett, Margaret Towers.

George Bannard on his horse. A caption on the back of the postcard says, 'Thrupp Grounds, Daventry, 11 September 1917. I am the old grey horse, the property of George Bannard. I am 30 years old, and for 28 years I have carried him faithfully. Now I am going to "do my bit" for the British Farmers' Red Cross [Daventry] Fund. I am going to be sold by auction but of course I go back to my old master at the finish of the sale and I hope, ladies and gentlemen, you will give me a good turn'.

Cattle struck by lightning, believed to be in Norton Park, early 1900s.

May Day celebrations, The Old Rectory, Crick, 1929. Left to right: Reg Fox, Bill Branston, Lilliam Lewis (seated), Madge Crofts, Elsie Warland (May Queen), Gwen Adnitt, Rose Groves (seated), Joyce Adnitt.

May Day celebrations, The Old Rectory, Crick, 1930s. The names as supplied by the donor of the photograph are, from left to right: Tom Ashby (pierrot with fiddle), Verona Loydall (Welsh lady), Joyce Adnitt (lady clown), George Branston (on the back row, in hat and ruff), Mrs Branston (back row, fourth from right in the large bonnet), John Marson (the drummer boy in the centre), Elsie Simms (in the centre of the second row, with her mouth open), Jean Mawby (in the bridge costume), Sam Fox (fourth from left on the second row).

Crick Band, otherwise known as 'The Drunken Eight'. Ex-Servicemen's Day, in the paddock opposite the old Co-op, High Street, Crick. The paddock was an area consisting partly of a field and partly of Tommy Jones' Garage; the area is now covered by 'The Paddocks' housing development. Ex-Servicemen's Day began with Crick Band leading a procession around the village beginning at the Royal Oak. Afterwards in the paddock there would be races and a tea. Back row, left to right: Bill Fox, Thomas Warland (Ticker), Perce Pratt, Billy Grey, Ray Simms, Jim Barford, 'old' Mr Barford. Front row, left to right: Reg Taylor, George Fox, Frank Grey.

Daventry Town Band, 1960, in Daventry Band Hall, Waterloo.

H. Catlin's Band, 1930s. Left to right: Ted Abbott, Percy Abbott, Mr Catlin, Jack Thornton, Alfred Thornton. It later became known as the Syncopaters' Dance Band.

Youth Club Fête, 1960s.

Merry Comrades Captain's Party, New Theatre, Northampton, 1948. At the right on the second row is Ron Osborne, father of Steve Osborne. The Merry Comrades were begun by 'Uncle Dick' Field on a children's page in the Mercury and Herald. They were organized as a charity to help local hospitals, mainly to buy radio systems for the wards, and raised a lot of money. There was a leader in every village or town known as a Captain. The idea was carried on by Uncle Dick's widow, 'Auntie Dick', until finally being wound up in the 1980s.

Meeting of the hounds in Market Square, early 1900s.

Meeting of the hounds in Market Square, early 1950s. Ron Osborne is the third from right facing the camera and stroking the dog. The figure among the hounds is 'Sweater' Cox.

George Bernard 'Sweater' Cox, sometime rag and bone man and town character. He was well known for his entertaining monologues.

May Day celebrations in the Market Square, 1960s.

Daventry Open Air Swimming Pool, Ashby Road, 1971.

Five

Celebrations
and Occasions

Ox roast for Queen Victoria's Diamond Jubilee (see p. 83). (see p. 83)

A typical group at Daventry, 1860. According to the inscription on the back of the photograph, the names (not in order) are 'Hinkes, Gent., Piddington, Cooke, Wright J., Bailey Geo., Wright Ed., ..., Hatfield, George, North'.

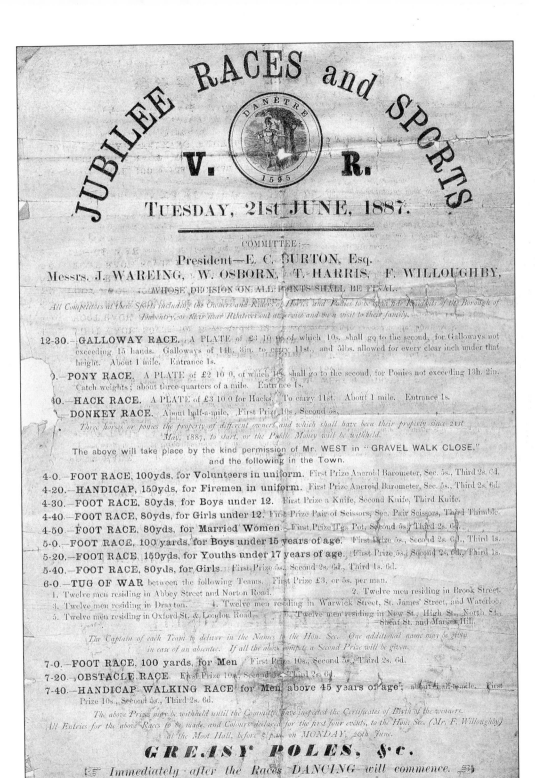

JUBILEE RACES and SPORTS

V. R.

TUESDAY, 21st JUNE, 1887.

COMMITTEE:—

President—E. C. BURTON, Esq.

Messrs. J. WAREING, W. OSBORN, T. HARRIS, F. WILLOUGHBY,
WHOSE DECISION ON ALL POINTS SHALL BE FINAL.

All Competitors at these Sports including the Owners and Riders of Horses and Ponies to be bonâ fide Residents of the Borough of Daventry, or their near Relatives out at service and on a visit to their family.

12-30.—GALLOWAY RACE. A PLATE of £3 10 0, of which 10s. shall go to the second, for Galloways not exceeding 15 hands. Galloways of 14h. 3in. to carry 11st., and 5lbs. allowed for every clear inch under that height. About 1 mile. Entrance 1s.

0.—PONY RACE. A PLATE of £2 10 0, of which 10s. shall go to the second, for Ponies not exceeding 13h. 2in. Catch weights; about three-quarters of a mile. Entrance 1s.

30.—HACK RACE. A PLATE of £3 10 0 for Hacks. To carry 11st. About 1 mile. Entrance 1s.

—DONKEY RACE. About half-a-mile. First Prize 10s., Second 5s.

Three horses or ponies the property of different owners and which shall have been their property since 21st May, 1887, to start, or the Public Money will be withheld.

The above will take place by the kind permission of Mr. WEST in "GRAVEL WALK CLOSE,"
and the following in the Town.

4-0.—FOOT RACE, 100yds, for Volunteers in uniform. First Prize Aneroid Barometer, Sec. 5s., Third 2s. 6d.

4-20.—HANDICAP, 150yds, for Firemen in uniform. First Prize Aneroid Barometer, Sec. 5s., Third 2s. 6d.

4-30.—FOOT RACE, 80yds, for Boys under 12. First Prize a Knife, Second Knife, Third Knife.

4-40.—FOOT RACE, 80yds, for Girls under 12. First Prize Pair of Scissors, Sec. Pair Scissors, Third Thimble.

4-50.—FOOT RACE, 80yds, for Married Women. First Prize Tea Pot, Second 5s., Third 2s. 6d.

5-0.—FOOT RACE, 100 yards, for Boys under 15 years of age. First Prize 5s., Second 2s. 6d., Third 1s.

5-20.—FOOT RACE, 150yds, for Youths under 17 years of age. First Prize 5s., Second 2s. 6d., Third 1s.

5-40.—FOOT RACE, 80yds, for Girls. First Prize 5s., Second 2s. 6d., Third 1s. 6d.

6-0.—TUG OF WAR between the following Teams. First Prize £3, or 5s. per man.

1. Twelve men residing in Abbey Street and Norton Road.   2. Twelve men residing in Brook Street.
3. Twelve men residing in Drayton.   4. Twelve men residing in Warwick Street, St. James' Street, and Waterloo.
5. Twelve men residing in Oxford St. & London Road.   6. Twelve men residing in New St., High St., North St., Sheaf St. and Market Hill.

The Captain of each Team to deliver in the Names to the Hon. Sec. One additional name may be given in case of an absentee. If all the above compete a Second Prize will be given.

7-0.—FOOT RACE, 100 yards, for Men. First Prize 10s., Second 5s., Third 2s. 6d.

7-20.—OBSTACLE RACE. First Prize 10s., Second 5s., Third 2s. 6d.

7-40.—HANDICAP WALKING RACE for Men, above 45 years of age; about half-a-mile. First Prize 10s., Second 5s., Third 2s. 6d.

The above Prizes may be withheld until the Committee have inspected the Certificates of Birth of the winners.

All Entries for the above Races to be made, and Colours declared for the first four events, to the Hon. Sec. (Mr. F. Willoughby) at the Moot Hall, before 5 p.m. on MONDAY, 20th June.

GREASY POLES, &c.

☞ *Immediately after the Races DANCING will commence.* ☜

J. W. BARRETT, PRINTER, ETC., DAVENTRY.

Poster advertising celebrations for Queen Victoria's Golden Jubilee, 1887.

Queen Victoria's Diamond Jubilee, July 1897. An old copy of the Daventry Express tells of 'the day the town went mad' and beat all previous records of 'rejoicings' by providing a free feast for 3,000 people in the High Street, the scene depicted above.

Queen Victoria's Diamond Jubilee, July 1897. This is a view of the High Street from the Market Square.

Basting one of the oxen roasted on the occasion of Queen Victoria's Diamond Jubilee in July 1897.

More festivities in High Street for Queen Victoria's Diamond Jubilee, 1897.

Feasting in Market Square for Queen Victoria's Diamond Jubilee, 1897.

More feasting in honour of Queen Victoria's Diamond Jubilee, this time in front of the Plume of Feathers.

End of a Memorial Service, probably for Edward VII, in Market Square, 20 May 1910.

Three soldiers in front of School House, Drayton, *c.* 1914.

From a Northampton newspaper of 4 May 1912, headed 'Motor Mobilisation at Daventry'. The caption reads: 'From left to right: Major Symonds, Captain Trapmann and General B. Thorneycroft. The motorist in the road facing the camera is Mr S. Gillingham of Suffolk, who rode 130 miles in four hours and one minute. Motorists for many miles round mobilised at Daventry on Saturday for a surprise test in connection with the Legion of Motorists and the event attracted a large number of interested spectators. Major-General Thorneycroft, who was in command, inspected and addressed the entrants, and spoke appreciatively of their value as dispatch carriers, but pointed out that except as messengers or guides they would be of little use in the event of war unless they had previous military training. The General subsequently witnessed the hill climbing tests held at Newnham Hill.' Apparently, the Legion's motorists offered their services as motorized cavalry. To convince the General of their usefulness, they gave a demonstration including a climb of Newnham Hill. The General concluded that he could see no practical purpose for motorcycles in wartime and limited use for cars except for staff transport!

The Royal Artillery lining New Street. The soldiers were on manoeuvres in the town in 1913 on land which is now the Long March industrial estate. The photograph was taken just outside 23 New Street and shows Mary Snart, mother of Harold Snart, and his two sisters, Elsie and Molly. F.C. Townsend in *Memories of Daventry in the Early 1900s* remembers when the manoeuvres were held and that King George and Queen Mary drove through the town, waving as the motorcade passed in New Street.

The Royal Artillery in Daventry, 1913.

A tank rounding the corner by Pytchley Motors on Sheaf Street.

A united gathering for praise and thanksgiving on Peace Day, 19 July 1919, in Market Square facing the Moot Hall.

The same gathering for Peace Day, facing New Street.

Getting a better view of Peace Day in Market Square.

The Rector giving a blessing in front of the Moot Hall, Market Square, probably at the time of the coronation of George VI in 1937.

The Mayor of Daventry reading the Queen's Proclamation from the Burton Memorial, 1952.

Vic Oliver, who was performing at the New Theatre, Northampton, visiting a munitions factory, 1942/3.

Claude Dampier, appearing locally with ENSA, visited the Wheatsheaf, 1944. He is shown here with Alec McGill.

Winston Churchill in the High Street during the election campaign in June 1945. Also present is Major R.E. Manningham-Buller, National Conservative candidate for the Daventry Division.

Clement Atlee (at the centre, holding the paper) pictured with Mrs Atlee (on his right) and a group of workers in Daventry during the 1945 election campaign.

Six
Churches and Schools

Pupil teacher and children from the British School (see p. 103).

West View of Daventry Priory, 1720s.

A priory of Cluniac monks, founded by Hugh de Leicester at Preston Capes in around 1090, moved to Daventry in 1107. Because it refused land to Cardinal Wolsey for his new college at Oxford, he dissolved the Priory in 1526. The buildings then decayed; Bridges, the county historian, noted in 1720 that nothing remained except a hall let to the landlord of The Swan which stood opposite the church. The old priory buildings were converted into a workhouse in 1826 but abandoned for this use when the new Union Workhouse was built in 1836/7 (now Danetre Hospital). The Abbey buildings are now the Ex-Servicemen's Club.

Holy Cross Church, Daventry, from the Market Square. The present parish church building was started in 1752 and finished in 1758. It is the only eighteenth-century town church in Northamptonshire.

The exterior of Holy Cross from the churchyard, early 1900s.

The interior of Holy Cross Church.

The old railings which surrounded the churchyard. The two people unsuitably dressed for the snowy day are perhaps on a break from the Stead & Simpson factory just down the road from the Church.

Miss Tina Winter, daughter of Canon J.F. Winter, who was Rector from 1933 to 1944, inspecting the bells when they were removed for repair in 1964/5.

Holy Cross Church at night, 1970.

St James' Church, Daventry, 1839. St James' Church which stood on St James Street was consecrated in 1840 as a chapel of ease to Holy Cross Church. It was opposite St James' School, and closed in 1958.

St James' Church, St James Street, at the far left. In the foreground are limousines belonging to Osborne's Taxis, a firm owned by Steve Osborne's grandparents.

Interior of St James' Church.

Wesleyan Methodist Church, New Street, Daventry, c. 1910. The Wesleyans first met in 1797 when their meetings were held in Cow Lane (now New Street) where their first meeting house was built in 1801. It was replaced by a new chapel in 1824 and in 1974 a new Methodist Church was built in Golding Close. The old chapel is now a night club.

Congregational Chapel, Sheaf Street, Daventry. The Independent congregation set up a chapel in a house and land in Sheaf Street in 1721. This is now the United Reformed Church and is the oldest church building in Daventry.

Interior of the Congregational Church.

The Grammar School, New Street, which became the Roman Catholic Church, then Windsor Lodge restaurant, and is now a private house. The Roman Catholic congregation in Daventry has met in various locations, including the old Grammar School which was leased and refurbished as a church dedicated to 'Our Lady of Charity and Saint Augustine' and was purchased in 1924. The present church is in London Road.

Altar in the Roman Catholic church, Daventry.

Children outside the buildings of the Abbey National School, founded in 1710 as Madras School and located in Market Square.

British School, Foundry Place, Daventry, c. 1891. On the extreme left of the picture is R.J. Willoughby (b. 1877, son of James Wesley Willoughby, see p. 38) who was a pupil teacher. According to Whellan's Directory for 1874, the British School was established in 1842 and was held in the Independent Sunday School, Foundry Place; it was supported by voluntary contributions and was well attended. The school must have acquired its own building because Kelly's Directory for 1903 says that the school (mixed) was built in Foundry Place in 1870 and enlarged in 1895; there was space for 242 children and the average attendance was 180. Frederick Billingham was the master.

The Grammar School, North Street, now the library.

The Grammar School for Girls, Bishop Crewe's Hostel, North Street, *c.* 1906.

St James' School, St James Street. The wall on the left of the picture divided the boys from the girls.

Grammar School House, Daventry.

Walking to Southbrook School, 1970.

Grange Primary School, mid-1970s.

Miss Summers, head teacher of St James' School (third from left), during Daventry Window Box Week, 1967.

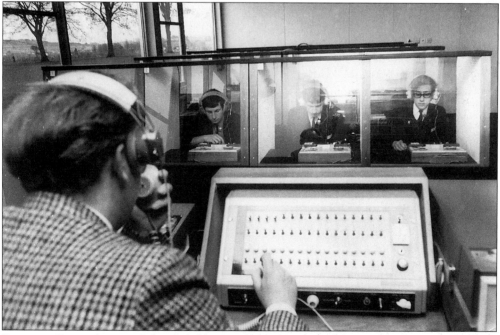

Daventry Comprehensive School, Ashby Road, 1960s.

Air Training Corps members at rifle drill, Drayton Manor Farm, *c.* 1970.

Air Training Corps radio instruction in the Radio Room, Drayton Manor Farm, 1960s-1970s.

Seven

All Change

Artist's impression of New Street (see p. 114).

In 1967, Northamptonshire County Council produced its written analysis of the Daventry Town Map. It states, 'The object of the Town Map is to provide for the expansion of Daventry to a total population of about 36,000 people by 1981. This very considerable expansion will be achieved by the reception of overspill population from Birmingham and natural increase'. Although the estimated population did not materialize, which is perhaps just as well for the sake of the present inhabitants (the population of Daventry in the 1991 census was approximately 18,000), there followed three decades of great change in and around the town. Because they have been so significant for the people of Daventry, this section illustrates some of these changes. What is remarkable, in a way, is how much of the town has been retained in a form which would be recognized by an eighteenth-century traveller.

Aerial view of Daventry town centre, 1967. The back of the police station and the recreation ground are in the foreground. London Road and Sheaf Street can be seen stretching northwards in the lower left hand corner.

Aerial view of Daventry from the south showing the Headlands estate and Long March industrial estate, 1968.

Aerial view of Headlands estate and Royal Oak industrial estate, 1968. Cummins' factory is on the left.

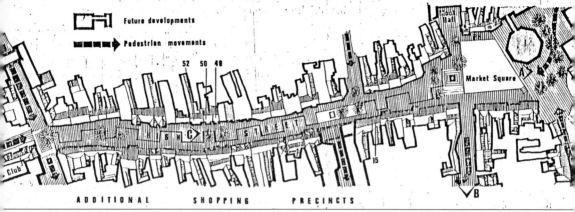

Plan of the redevelopment of the High Street showing the viewpoints for the artist's impressions which follow.

Birmingham Public Works Department artist's impression of Market Square, 1968 (A on plan above).

Market Square, *c*. 1965.

Birmingham Public Works Department artist's impression of New Street looking towards the Moot Hall, 1968 (B on plan, p. 112).

General view of New Street, *c.* 1965.

Birmingham Public Works Department artist's impression of High Street, looking towards the BBC Club, 1968 (C on plan, p. 112).

'High Street' by Chris Searle, February 1964.

'Brook Street' by Chris Searle, February 1964.

Brook Street closed for alteration, c. 1965.

The BBC Club on the corner of Sheaf
Street and Tavern Lane, 1975.

'Sheaf Street' by Chris Searle, February
1964.

'Braunston Road' by Chris Searle, February 1964.

Braunston Road service station near the Royal Oak pub at the beginning of work to build Ford's works, 1966.

'London Road' by Chris Searle, April 1964.

'Expanding Town' by Chris Searle: a view of Daventry from Borough Hill in April 1963.

Construction of Eastern Way, 1967.

Construction of Manor Road and St Augustin Way, 1967.

Waterloo and the gasometer, 1967.

View of Daventry from Borough Hill
showing what is reputed to be the
Dane tree.

Railway station and stationmaster's house, 1960s.

Pest House Lane, February 1967. This is now the site of Cummins' car park.

Borough Hill and BBC masts from the end of Abbey Street, April 1972.

Burnt Walls, 1966.

The Lord Mayor of Birmingham, Alderman H.E. Tyler, and the Mayor of Daventry, Councillor George Tutcher. This ceremony was held on 13 December 1966 for the first of sixty-one trees planted on Long March to mark the affiliation of the Daventry Tree Lovers' Association to the Birmingham City League. The children represent six schools, ten from each school, and each child planted one tree.

Green Shield Trading Stamp Company shop display on Daventry in the Bull Ring in Birmingham, 1970.

Exhibition entitled 'People on the Move' held in the Bull Ring in Birmingham, 1968.

New Street Recreation Ground, 1970. The old locomotive engine is from the old ironstone quarry at Byfield, used to transport stone from there to Charwelton until the quarry closed in 1965. The inscription indicates that the picture was intended to encourage people to live in Daventry.

Cunningham Close, c. 1970. Another enticement to Daventry life.

Opposite: The engine is obviously popular with the local lads.

Acknowledgements

When the idea of compiling this book of photographs of Daventry was suggested to me, I knew that it could not be done without the help of the Daventry Museum and it was there that I went first. Victoria Gabbitas, the curator, was immediately enthusiastic and supportive and it is photographs from the museum's collection which form the basis of the book. My special thanks go to Mrs Gabbitas who has written the introduction and to the Charter Trustees of Daventry for their permission to use the photographs from that collection.

I also consulted the Northamptonshire Record Office and discovered the Phipps Brewery collection which includes many photographs of Daventry pubs. Permission was willingly given by the Record Office for their use. Copies were made by Peter Moyse of Helpston, member of The Association of Historical and Fine Art Photography, whom it is difficult to thank enough for his help.

But the pleasure I have had in gathering the photographs for this book has been due mainly to the people of Daventry whom I have met and who have lent me photographs. The trail began with Steve Osborne who put me in touch with John Brown, Dave Liddington and Rick Willoughby. All of their collections are fascinating and they have all enthusiastically lent photographs for the book.

Through them I learned about Mrs Betty Thornton who was also very willing to allow some photos from her well known collection to be used. From Miss Tina Winter I gained not only photographs but many wonderful stories which have enhanced the book. The trail also led to Mrs 'Bobby' Hughes who has a superb collection through which she encouraged me to browse and use what I needed. At a meeting of the Daventry and District Society I met Mr and Mrs John Harding who very kindly gave me a copy of the photograph of Jack Harding. Chris Searle contacted me as a result of my plea in the Daventry Express and a number of his own photographs as well as some wonderful historic pictures from his collection grace the book. The people at White & Co. kindly let me use a photograph from an old brochure.

Another obvious source of photographs is the local newspaper and I am very grateful to the Express for putting pleas for help in the 'Gusher' and for putting me in touch with Pete Spencer who looked out some good old photographs. Writer and photographer Alan Burman has been more than generous in helping me with both his time and his vast collection, particularly with those relating to his special interest in motorcycles and cars. Aerofilms Ltd allowed me to use the aerial photograph on p. 10. Daventry Library is a mine of information on the town.

Everyone I have met over the months of compiling this book has been helpful and enthusiastic. I thank them all and hope that the book lives up to their expectations. Because I am sure I have missed some interesting photographs and would like to think that this book is only the beginning of an archive of Daventry historical photographs, I or Mrs Gabbitas would be very happy to hear from anyone else who has old photographs they would be willing to share with others. I would also like to hear of any errors of fact which need to be corrected.

Finally, my thanks to my husband, Peter, for his patience and support and to David Buxton and his colleagues at Chalford Publishing for the same and for making me feel at home on my several visits to St Mary's Mill.